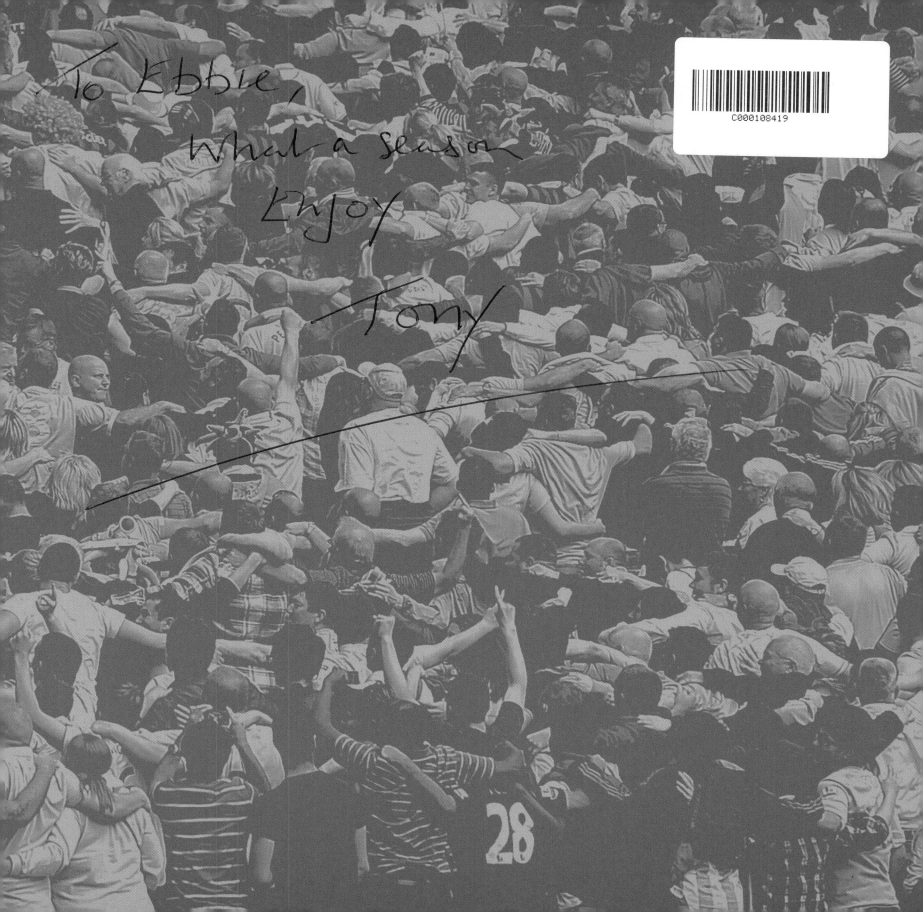

To Ebbie,
What a season
Enjoy

Tony

28

To Eddie, enjoy memories of our great season Tony

#CHAMPIONS
UNCUT

THE PASSION.

THE GLORY.

THE REAL STORY OF OUR SEASON IN PICTURES

OFFICIAL LICENSED PRODUCT

Sport Media

A Trinity Mirror Business

Images: Sharon Latham
Words: David Clayton
Cover design and overall layout: Colin Sumpter
Production: Roy Gilfoyle

Produced by Trinity Mirror Sport Media

Executive Editor: Ken Rogers. Senior Editor: Steve Hanrahan
Senior Production Editor: Paul Dove. Senior Art Editor: Rick Cooke

Business Development Manager: Will Beedles
Sales and Marketing Manager: Elizabeth Morgan
Sales and Marketing Assistant: Karen Cadman
Marketing Executive: Claire Brown

First Edition
Published in Great Britain in 2012 by: Trinity Mirror Sport Media,
PO Box 48, Old Hall Street, Liverpool L69 3EB.
Copyright of Manchester City Football Club.

ISBN: 9781908695376

Additional photography: PA Photos

Printed by KINT Ljubljana

16

30

90

108

140

162

48

62

74

122

182

CONTENTS

THIS BOOK EVOKES GREAT MEMORIES OF A GREAT YEAR. SHARON'S PICTURES PORTRAY THE SPIRIT, THE PROFESSIONALISM AND THE CHARACTER OF MANCHESTER CITY

I am very happy that this book has been made and that all of our fans will have a very special souvenir with which they can remember the way Manchester City won its first title in 44 years.

We are lucky at the club that we have someone as dedicated to her work as our club photographer Sharon Latham who is with the squad nearly every day taking the pictures that you will see in this book.

She has quickly become part of the team and has great respect from everyone who works at the club.

We are very proud at City that we are a close team off the field as well as on it and that's why there are so many unique photographs in this book.

They vividly show not only the day-to-day life at our training centre both for footballers and staff, but also the emotion of the season beyond match day.

The book captures our journey from the pre-season to the last day of the Premier League campaign when we were crowned champions. It was a day that made history and will be remembered by our fans for many years to come. Now they have this fantastic record of the best moments.

Sharon is a big part of the team documenting the life in our workplace with her cameras. Her pictures portray the spirit, the professionalism, the fun and the character of Manchester City and I am sure you will agree that this book evokes great memories of a great year.

I think it is probably true to say that in the twenty years of its existence the Barclays Premier League has never experienced such a crazy or fantastic season.

For us at Manchester City the 2011-12 title win was truly historic and we have always dedicated it to our fantastic fans, many of whom were not born or who were very young when their favourites were last champions of England.

That is why I am sure that the supporters will enjoy this book very much. There were many great moments over 10 long months but some that will inevitably have been forgotten in the minds of some people. I am sure these photographs will serves as a great way of jogging the memory.

I hope you all enjoy smiling your way through the pages as much as I did.

Thank you Sharon.

FOREWORD BY ROBERTO MANCINI
Manchester City FC title-winning manager

VINCENT KOMPANY

Manchester City FC title-winning captain

"Our title win was amazing and one of the best feelings ever for us and the fans. That last game against QPR will be a very special part of City's history for the next 50 or 100 years.

"I have travelled a lot all over the world and our story has been a big story everywhere. It made a huge impact.

"We have laid the foundations and now we want to win more. If we do that then we can be one of the most successful clubs for a long time to come and that is the aim."

IT'S FANTASTIC THAT WE HAVE A PICTORIAL ACCOUNT OF THE SEASON BECAUSE THINGS HAPPENED SO FAST. I CAN'T REALLY REMEMBER ANY OF IT! IT'S ALL JUST A BLUR NOW, BUT A HAPPY BLUR ALL THE SAME

The reason the pictures in this book are so good and, at times, so off the beaten track is simple – we, the players, trust Sharon... and that's something money can't buy.

Put simply, if the trust wasn't there, we would be cagey around her, wondering where the pictures that had been taken might eventually end up.

That might sound a little strange, but as a professional footballer, sometimes a person pointing a camera at you doesn't always have your best intentions at heart and that can put you on your guard. If you're on guard you won't be relaxed and you won't get the sort of

pictures Sharon has in the pages that follow.

It's fantastic that we have a pictorial account of last season because things happened so fast. I can't really remember any of it! It's all just a blur now, but a happy blur all the same.

I don't have one particular picture I cherish more than another. I like them all, but there are a few I wouldn't mind on my mantelpiece. They're in here, somewhere!

So I hope you enjoy re-living last season as much as I did. It's confined to the history books now, of course. This is one of them – as we try and write some more history in the years to come.

JOE HART
Manchester City FC title-winning goalkeeper

THE WHISTLE WENT AND THE TITLE WAS OURS. IT WAS INCREDIBLE. UNBELIEVABLE. IMPOSSIBLE.

Some things, they say, are written in the stars. The events of the 2011/12 season suggest City's destiny was decided before a ball was even kicked – it just felt like this was our year, our time… our turn.

Roberto Mancini had fine-tuned his squad, but not made wholesale changes. Sergio Aguero had arrived from Atletico Madrid and Samir Nasri would also join a week or so into the new season. Stefan Savic would provide useful cover in the centre of defence, but otherwise, that was it.

Nobody shouted it from the rooftops, but after finishing fifth and third in the previous two seasons, City felt they were ready to really challenge for the title. The FA Cup triumph had ended a 36-year wait for silverware and proved that this squad was capable of great things.

The question was, could they maintain a challenge from the first to the last day of the campaign? Consistency would be the key, belief the mantra but it was hard work and desire that would be needed in abundance to see off the likes of Manchester United, Tottenham, Chelsea and Arsenal.

The Blues needed to hit the ground running and make an early statement and the Community Shield offered the perfect opportunity to do just that. Manchester United at Wembley – was there a better platform to show the world that City meant business?

Goals from Joleon Lescott and Edin Dzeko gave the Blues a 2-0 half-time lead, but United fought back after the break to pull level and when Nani grabbed an injury-time winner, an important lesson had been learned. It wasn't so much a wake-up call, more of a reminder of the task ahead.

So to the opening day of the campaign and a home match against newly-promoted Swansea. The Swans proved stubborn opposition, playing expansive football that could have seen them go ahead as City sought to gain a foothold, but eventually the Blues edged ahead and after establishing a two-goal lead, Sergio Aguero came off the bench to add the icing to the cake with a goal moments after his introduction and another not long after to complete a 4-0 opening day win.

It was the perfect start and it set the scene for the months ahead.

A hard-fought 3-2 win at Bolton secured a first three points on the road, but what followed away to Tottenham stunned the rest of the Premier League as the Blues swept aside one of their title challengers with a breathless display of stunning football. Edin Dzeko bagged four in a 5-1 victory at White Hart Lane.

While the City fans were still celebrating, news filtered through that United had beaten Arsenal 8-2 – the battle of Manchester had begun in earnest and would run until the very last kick of the season.

By the time the first league Manchester derby of the campaign arrived, the Blues were playing imperious football. A win at Old Trafford would widen the gap at the top and also give Mancini's side the confidence they needed to have a strong autumn and head into November and December in a very strong position.

What happened didn't only confirm the Blues were worthy of wrestling the title from United, it proved City were the best team in Manchester.

Beating United 6-1 in their own backyard was a bitter pill for Reds fans to swallow and it led to a back-to-basics mentality from Sir Alex's side, while City marched on, winning the next five games in all competitions before Napoli all but ended Champions League hopes with a 2-1 win in Naples.

The Blues were soon back in their stride, winning three and drawing one of the next four before Chelsea became the first Premier League team to record a win over City with a controversial 2-1 victory at Stamford Bridge.

How would the team respond to the first loss? Wins over Stoke City and Arsenal answered that particular question.

But January would test the nerves of players, manager and supporters. Sunderland clung on for 93 minutes at the Stadium of Light in the first game of 2012 – and then stole all three points with an offside goal, but a sparkling 3-0 win over Liverpool restored the faith.

Yaya and Kolo Toure would then depart for the African Cup of Nations and the Blues would endure a testing few weeks, seeing their unbeaten home record go in a 3-2 FA Cup defeat to United and then Liverpool won 1-0 in the Carling Cup semi-final first

leg at the Etihad Stadium. Worse still, skipper Vincent Kompany was banned for four games following his dismissal against the Reds and City were plunged into a defensive crisis ahead of vital games against Wigan and Spurs.

A hard-fought 1-0 win over the Latics brought a welcome three points, but perhaps the most pivotal moment of the season came in the next game against Spurs. Despite going 2-0 up, Tottenham fought back to 2-2 and looked set to become the first side to pick up a point against City at the Etihad. Then Gareth Bale broke down the left, crossed in low and Jermain Defoe seemed certain to win the game – but he slid the ball wide by a fraction.

Then City went up the other end and Mario Balotelli won and scored an injury-time penalty that gave the Blues a crucial three points.

City won their next four league games, but it seemed United had timed their run to perfection as the Blues lost at Swansea, drew at Stoke and then drew at home to Sunderland. Seven points had been frittered away and United were now five clear.

Victory at Arsenal seemed an absolute must with United playing at home the same afternoon, but a late Mikel Arteta goal and a win for United looked to have finally ended City's challenge. Eight points adrift and just six games left… United were home and hosed.

The City players were down, but they never stopped believing. Interviewing a solemn James Milner after the game, he told me: "We just need to win our last six matches and see where it takes us. That's all we can do."

What nobody could have known was a glimmer of hope would come in the next set of fixtures, with City beating West Brom 4-0 and the Reds losing to Wigan.

The Blues thrashed Norwich 6-1 at Carrow Road to take a healthy lead over the Reds in the goal difference stakes, and though United won their game, the next weekend would see another shock result as the Reds let a 4-2 lead against Everton slip in the final moments to draw 4-4. A 2-0 win at Wolves meant the gap was down to three ahead of the biggest Manchester derby of all time.

A victory would put City back on top of the table with only two games remaining – surely United couldn't fail again? Vincent Kompany's thumping header proved to be enough on the night and the Manchester clubs swapped places just a few yards short of the finishing line.

Of course, the drama didn't end there. A tense and tight match away to Newcastle seemed to be heading towards a 0-0 draw until two Yaya Toure goals sent the travelling City fans wild and the first chorus of 'We're gonna win the league!' was heard at St James' Park. One more win and the title was ours.

City, with by far and away the best home record, faced QPR who had one of the worst records in the Premier League. Surely it was as good as over?

Pablo Zabaleta settled the nerves of the capacity crowd with a goal before the break, but it was merely the calm before the storm. Rangers, needing a point to guarantee survival, equalised just after half-time through Djibril Cisse before Joey Barton saw red for elbowing Carlos Tevez.

But 10-man Rangers then broke and went ahead through Jamie Mackie – suddenly, with United winning at Sunderland, the title dream was over. City had to find two goals from somewhere – anywhere!

But as the clock ticked past 90 and into the five minutes of added time, it seemed impossible that City could turn the game around. A corner on 91 minutes saw sub Edin Dzeko make it 2-2 and as Sky Sports commentator Martin Tyler said: "It's simple. One goal and City win the title."

With added time just seconds from completion, Sergio Aguero picked the ball up 30 yards from goal, nudged it to Balotelli who held off his marker and rolled the ball back into Aguero's path. The Argentine feigned to shoot, nudged it past the defender and then fired the ball past Paddy Kenny to make it 3-2 and send the Etihad Stadium into a frenzied celebration, the like of which we will probably never see again.

The whistle went and the title was ours. It was incredible. Unbelievable. Impossible.

This is the behind the scenes story of the greatest title victory of all time, seen through the lens of club photographer Sharon Latham.

Now, enjoy the journey all over again.

DAVID CLAYTON
Official Manchester City FC
club content producer

THE PLAYERS SEE ME AS PART OF THE FURNITURE.
THEIR PERSONALITIES COME OUT THE MORE THEY RELAX

I've been taking photographs for more than 35 years and I feel honoured and privileged to be Manchester City's official club photographer. I've been at City for nearly four years and the 2011/12 campaign was an amazing, emotional rollercoaster of a season, culminating with the team winning the Premier League title for the first time in 44 years.

I was lucky enough to be there every step of the way and I hope that this collection of images helps everyone see a more intimate side to what went on behind the scenes and away from public view.

Part of the reason I've been able to produce this book is down to the amazing access I am granted by Roberto Mancini, David Platt and the playing staff of this wonderful football club. Without their consent, I'd have just the usual training shots and match action.

Having a camera constantly in your face can be rather off-putting, but luckily the players are so used to having me around they now see me as part of the furniture, which means I'm able to snap candidly and the players are relaxed with me doing so.

In fact, the players' personalities come out the more they relax and at Manchester City, we have some fantastic personalities - trust me!

If you enjoy this book half as much as I enjoyed taking the pictures then I will have done my job.

I've had to wade through literally thousands of images to find the very best of the bunch. Most have never been seen before and each has a meaning behind it as the story of a glorious season is told from pre-season through to the open top bus tour around Manchester.

The way the lads are going, I'd better start collating for #Champions Uncut II straight away...

SHARON LATHAM
Official Manchester City FC
club photographer

Ready for take-off

With the 2011/12 season on approach, several members of the first-team squad attend a photo shoot at Manchester Airport where the brand new Etihad Airways liveried A330-200 jet is unveiled for the first time. A relaxed knockabout on the tarmac as jumbos speed by – not your average training session…

BACK IN BUSINESS

Joe Hart is one of the first players to report back for pre-season training at Carrington.

Still wearing flip-flops, the England keeper is in relaxed mode before the real work begins.

He is also set to be joined by two new team-mates in Stefan Savic (top) and Gael Clichy (above).

With just a couple of days to go before the team flies to the US, there won't be anything too strenuous in store for Joe and the rest of the squad.

Drinks breaks were essential in the midday sun as Adam Johnson takes a chance to top up his Teesside tan

UCLA ALL THE WAY

Under blue skies and warm summer sunshine, the players assemble for the opening training session of the US tour at the UCLA campus in Santa Monica.

With perfect facilities and surroundings, the first few sessions begin with the aim of building up stamina through a series of strengthening exercises.

Here Joe Hart plays up to the camera as he and Stuart Taylor practise claiming corner kicks while David Silva tests Shaun Wright-Phillips' sports bra!

PITCHER PERFECT

Joe Hart is the invited guest of LA Dodgers to throw the opening pitch during a day off for the players. Of course, Joe threw a curve ball…

The City keeper was clearly enjoying his pre-season tour as he entertained his team-mates in a hotel room.

David Silva took a break from the intense heat while Micah Richards chilled out, but was there a subliminal message in the hills?

Classic car collector Nigel de Jong tests his driving skills with Roberto Mancini trying a bit of pinball

CAGED TIGERS

There was never a dull moment on the US tour. Whether it was a trip to the HQ of EA Sports in Vancouver to test out some classic arcade games or a sample of the life of a UFC cage fighter, the players enjoyed every minute of the North American training camp.

There was even a warm-up in the hotel lobby in San Francisco prior to the opening game against Club America where the action finally began in earnest at AT&T Park.

Joleon Lescott pins down Micah Richards in what looks more like a wrestling move while Patrick Vieira and Nigel de Jong enjoy the Richards-Lescott tussle

An event for local kids at Long Beach was also a chance for
Aleks Kolarov and Edin Dzeko to catch some rays. Hundreds of
local schoolchildren gave the players a fantastic welcome before
James Milner and Gareth Barry took part in a spot of beach football

A GALAXY FAR FAR AWAY

City take on David Beckham's LA Galaxy in the final match of the tour.
   Played in front of a huge crowd at the Home Depot Arena, the game
ends in a draw but City win on penalties with Joe Hart successfully
converting one – much to the delight of Aleks Kolarov.
   If anything, Hart was even happier when he met a couple of Hollywood
A-listers in Demi Moore and Ashton Kutcher.

SIGN OF THE TIMES

Sergio Aguero arrives in Manchester to sign for City.

The former Atletico Madrid striker is one of the brightest talents in world football and after being greeted by a large crowd of supporters at the Etihad Stadium, Sergio was happy to stop and sign dozens of autographs.

Aguero added a new dynamic to City's attack with the mouth-watering prospect of a double Argentine strike force with Carlos Tevez.

Start of the journey

August was a month for putting the final pieces of the jigsaw together with Samir Nasri the highest profile of the club's signings ahead of the transfer deadline. The season began with a trip to Wembley while a marathon league campaign got off to a fast start

FIXTURES

AUG 7......C SHIELD....N
MAN UTD   2-3

AUG 15......PL.....HOME
SWANSEA   4-0

AUG 21......PL.....AWAY
BOLTON   3-2

AUG 28......PL.....AWAY
TOTTENHAM   5-1

OPEN TRAINING DAY

Nigel de Jong signs a shirt during an open training session at the Etihad Stadium.

The club have always been keen to make the players as accessible as possible with this annual event popular with supporters and particularly youngsters who get the opportunity to see their heroes (such as Mario Balotelli) up close.

Meanwhile, Carrington life (left) is relaxed as the sharpness returns.

Micah Richards pedals a few kilometres, Gareth Barry checks up on his emails and Patrick Vieira deals with an admin issue with the help of Clare Marsden, PA to the manager and chief football operations officer.

NEXT STOP WEMBLEY

The boys set off from Stockport train station for Wembley
and the Community Shield curtain-raiser against Manchester
United.

It's an opportunity to meet supporters, surf the net on their
iPads and smartphones or simply assist with the operating of
a new Blackberry!

Either way, with an FA Cup in the trophy cabinet and
Champions League football to look forward to, the mood is
clearly relaxed and happy.

The Community Shield proves to be a thrilling game, but City blow a 2-0 lead to lose 3-2. Joleon Lescott and Edin Dzeko are City's scorers on a day that ultimately proves to be something of an anti-climax

Manchester United 2-3 Wembley

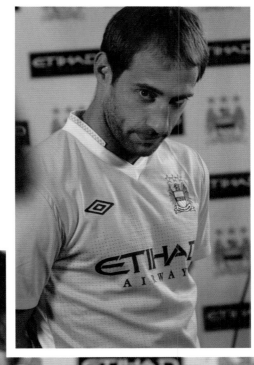

ONE FOR THE CAMERA

Sky Sports' walk-in shots are always left as late as possible before the Premier League campaign begins to accommodate any last-minute signings.

With a green screen for a backdrop, the players have to do several takes in both the home and away kits ready for transmission by mid-August.

Here, three Argentine amigos nail it in one – Pablo Zabaleta, Carlos Tevez and Sergio Aguero.

FRIENDLY FAREWELL

City said goodbye to a couple of crowd favourites before the transfer window closed.

Craig Bellamy earned a dream move to his boyhood favourites Liverpool after spending the previous season at Cardiff City and Shaun Wright-Phillips left the Blues for London for a second time, signing for QPR on this occasion.

Aleks Kolarov looks like a man who's been caught in the act as he sits in a golf buggy at Carrington

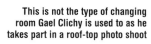

This is not the type of changing room Gael Clichy is used to as he takes part in a roof-top photo shoot

PLAY IT AGAIN, SAMIR

Samir Nasri became the last part of Roberto Mancini's jigsaw when he signed for City from Arsenal.

The gifted midfielder had grown tired of life at Arsenal and resented the accusations he'd joined the Blues for purely financial reasons. "To all my critics, I say this: ask me again why I joined City at the end of the season. I'm here to win trophies."

He would fit into the Blues' system like a glove and was involved in three of City's goals on his debut at Tottenham. He would become an integral member of the team and, true to his word, he ended the season with exactly what he'd come for – a Premier League winners' medal.

Samir Nasri looks at home in his new surroundings as coach Attilio Lombardo learns not to tangle with Mario Balotelli

City made a real statement of intent as they thrashed Spurs at White Hart Lane with Edin Dzeko hitting four goals

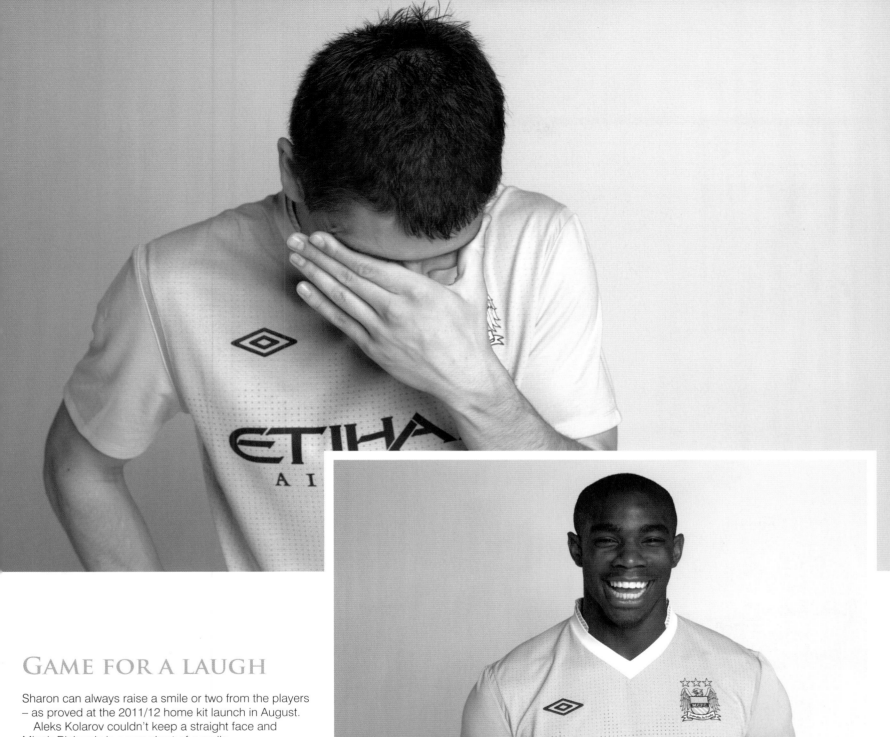

GAME FOR A LAUGH

Sharon can always raise a smile or two from the players
– as proved at the 2011/12 home kit launch in August.
   Aleks Kolarov couldn't keep a straight face and
Micah Richards is never short of a smile.
   There was plenty to be happy about, too, as City
blew away Spurs and Bolton on the road and opened
the campaign with a 4-0 thrashing of Swansea to
finish August in second spot and with 12 goals scored
already.

Follow the leader

An inspirational team needs an inspirational captain. At several points in the 2011/12 season City needed their talisman to step up to the plate and he never let his team-mates down, leading by example on the pitch and on the training ground

FIXTURES

SEP 10........PL......HOME
WIGAN   3-0

SEP 14........CL......HOME
NAPOLI   1-1

SEP 18........PL......AWAY
FULHAM   2-2

SEP 21........LC......HOME
BIRMINGHAM 2-0

SEP 24........PL......HOME
EVERTON   2-0

SEP 27........PL......AWAY
BAY. MUNICH   0-2

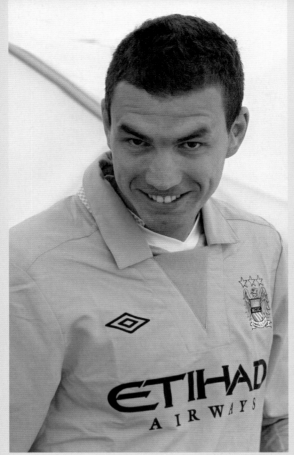

SERG-ING PAST LATICS

A confident City took on Wigan Athletic at the Etihad Stadium. Sergio Aguero would go on to claim his first match ball with a hat-trick in the 3-0 victory that kept the Blues in second, separated from pole position by a slightly inferior goal difference to Manchester United.

ALEKS THE GREAT

Serbian full-back Aleks Kolarov arrived at City with a reputation for thunderous free-kicks – one knocked a referee unconscious earlier in his career.

He wrote his name into the club's history books with City's first goal in Champions League football when he netted an equaliser in the 1-1 draw with Napoli.

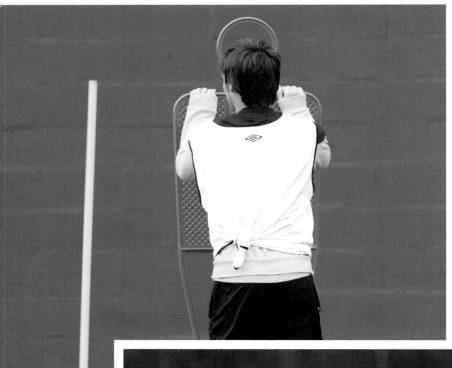

SOLID SILVA

David Silva began the season with numerous assists and a series of dazzling displays that would earn him numerous personal awards such as the Etihad Player of the Month, the Barclays Premier League Player of the Month for September and the Match! Player of the Month.

The brilliant Spaniard would be the beating heart of the Blues' title bid with his vision and trickery making him one of the first names on Roberto Mancini's team sheet.

Edin Dzeko's always got a smile for the camera – even in the middle of a tough training session

The main Man

Roberto Mancini never misses a training session and often joins in games.

A gifted forward during his playing days with Sampdoria, he's still got a trick or two up his sleeve, even though he's occasionally on the end of a rough tackle or two!

Even when the team warms up, the gaffer is there casting his eye over events – very much a 'hands-on' style of management.

City on Easy Street

Any title race will provide obstacles but in the month of October, every hurdle was comfortably cleared by Roberto Mancini's men. Six wins out of six in all competitions, scoring 24 goals in the process and beating our biggest rivals 6-1 on their own patch demonstrated the supreme confidence in the City camp

FIXTURES

OCT 01........PL....AWAY
BLACKBURN   4-0

OCT 15........PL....HOME
ASTON VILLA   4-1

OCT 18........CL....HOME
VILLARREAL   2-1

OCT 23........PL....AWAY
MAN UTD   6-1

OCT 26........LC....AWAY
WOLVES   5-2

OCT 29........PL....HOME
WOLVES   3-1

Every facial expression is covered as the players – or some of them at least – appear to be enjoying training with kit manager Les Chapman and masseur Carlo Sertori looking on

REACHING TOP GEAR

City powered to the top of the table with a 4-1 win over Aston Villa – despite resting several big names.

The strength of the squad proved to be the envy of the Premier League and whichever team Mancini played impressed and scored goals.

With the knock-out stages of the Champions League already looking like a tall order, the Blues now had their eyes firmly set on a first league title for 44 years.

Gareth Barry looks comfortable during a photo session in the John Rylands Library in Manchester

TENSION-FREE DERBY BUILD-UP

Top of the world and seemingly without a care in the world, the Blues' run-up to the first Manchester league derby of the season couldn't have been more relaxed with Roberto Mancini taking time out to do this airport lounge photo shoot.

And it was a novelty for City fans to travel to Old Trafford with their team looking down the table at United – something all Blues could definitely get used to!

MANCHESTER UNITED
MANCHESTER CITY

The scoreline says it all on a red letter day for City and the Premier League. Never has the Poznan been danced with such ecstasy

The City boys are in demand as Joe Hart conducts an interview while Gareth Barry shares the mic with EDS player Sean Tse, flanked by two Academy youngsters having their first taste of being in the limelight

Micah Richards and Mario Balotelli are in good spirits ahead of a comfortable home win against Wolves

EARLY SIGNS ARE GOOD

Sergio Aguero had become an instant hit with the City fans and hundreds turned out to attend a shirt signing at the new Market Street City Store.

With 10 goals already under his belt by early October, his signing from Atletico Madrid was looking an inspired move by the Blues. He was also clearly enjoying life in Manchester…

Life on the road

City faced a test of endurance during November with five of their six games away from home. It would turn out to be a profitable month, despite the travelling, with four wins and a draw spoiled only by a 2-1 defeat in Napoli

74

FIXTURES

NOV 02......CL......AWAY		
VILLARREAL	3-0	
NOV 05......PL......AWAY		
QPR	3-2	
NOV 19......PL......HOME		
NEWCASTLE	3-1	
NOV 22......CL......AWAY		
NAPOLI	1-2	
NOV 27......PL......AWAY		
LIVERPOOL	1-1	
NOV 29......LC......AWAY		
ARSENAL	1-0	

The team were based in Valencia for the Champions League match with Villarreal and, responding to a challenge, kit manager Les Chapman ended up in the hotel water feature

Missing his own dog Lucky, Mario Balotelli stopped to pet a local dog that was being walked at the time

GAIN IN SPAIN

The Villarreal trip proved a welcome escape from the rain of Manchester with the players taking a stroll down the Valencia promenade in the hazy mid-morning sun.

City won the game against Villarreal at a canter by three goals to nil with Yaya Toure scoring twice and Mario Balotelli netting from the spot.

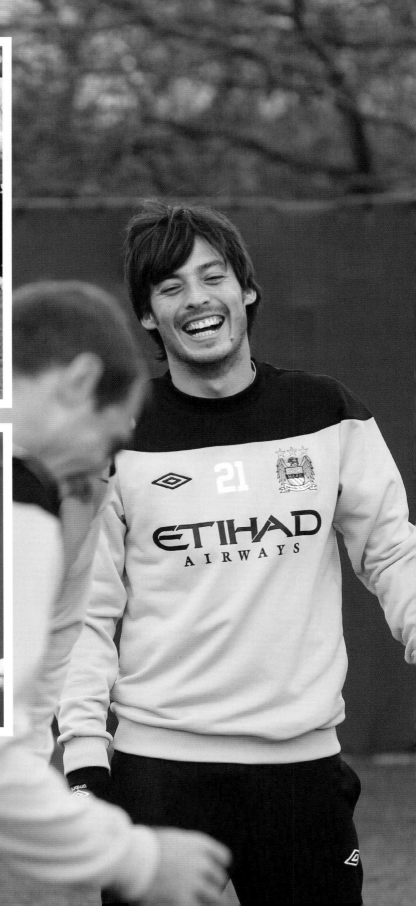

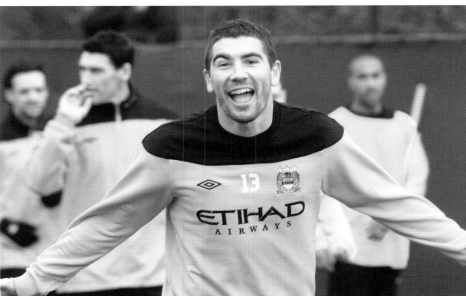

Clearly a happy camp, City
followed their 3-2 win at QPR with
a welcome home match against
Newcastle. There were plenty of
smiles during training as the Blues
continued to set the pace at the top
of the Premier League

HOME COMFORTS

A 3-1 home win over an in-form Newcastle United continued the Blues' 100 per cent home record with City comprehensively taking apart Alan Pardew's side.

Considering it was the only game at the Etihad Stadium in November, the home supporters made the most of it!

James Milner signs a young fan's shirt at a supporters club meeting while club cat Wimblydon awaits his morning feed outside the Carrington reception

HIGH-FLYING CITY'S CABIN FEVER

Air travel is part and parcel of the modern footballer's life, but it seemed at times City were in the air more often than they were on terra firma.

Most of the players either watch a film or play games on their iPads to pass the time, as on this flight to Napoli where a 2-1 defeat left the Blues' Champions League hopes hanging by a thread.

MEN OF THE PEOPLE

A walk through Naples drew hundreds of curious locals, many eager to see fellow Italians Roberto Mancini and Mario Balotelli.

With Napoli's reputation for creating a hostile atmosphere during their home games, Mancini was also keen to get the players in among the people to perhaps calm any nerves on the morning of the match.

Gael Clichy and Stefan Savic find time to pose for the camera but it was a difficult night on the pitch in Napoli

Where did we go wrong? The manager and Gael Clichy check in with the video analysis team back in Manchester

SLICE OF THE ACTION

Nigel de Jong celebrates his birthday with a slice of cake in the dining area at Carrington. A CityTV cameraman captures everything for the club's fly-on-the-wall documentary Inside City.

Also caught on camera is the moment Mario Balotelli claims his Etihad Player of the Month award from a young fan.

A true blue Christmas

City continued to set the pace during December, but a first Premier League defeat of the season suggested that Mancini's side were only human after all. The Blues would largely enjoy the festive period and would go into the new year still leading the table despite the end of their Champions League adventure

FIXTURES

Dec 03......PL......Home
NORWICH 5-1

Dec 07......CL......Home
BAY. MUNICH 2-0

Dec 12......PL......Away
CHELSEA 1-2

Dec 18......PL......Home
ARSENAL 1-0

Dec 21......PL......Home
STOKE CITY 3-0

Dec 26......PL......Away
WBA 0-0

91

HIGHLY DECORATED PLAYERS

Christmas now means cake-making for the players with their creative efforts auctioned off for the club's charities.

Vincent Kompany took particular pride in his masterpiece, with CityTV producer Michael Russell capturing his every move.

Meanwhile, Pablo Zabaleta (left) adheres to the old belief that if the hat fits, you should wear it, as Roberto Mancini, Nigel de Jong and Gael Clichy all join in the fun.

Sergio Aguero decides to sample the cake decorations. Considering he was the icing on the cake this season, nobody argued. David Silva's artistry is evident on and off the pitch...

the black dotted line below fo
along the red dotted line
for a star-shaped profile

ut higher or lower
to adjust
the piping size.

A 5-1 win over Norwich, inspired by the magical boots of David Silva, could have ended in double figures had the Blues finished all their chances

POOL OF TALENT

Mario Balotelli sharpens his pool skills in the recreation area at Carrington after arriving early for training.

These pictures of Mario, Kolo Toure and Micah Richards demonstrate that the clothing got warmer for the players as winter started to bite as they arrived at their training base.

MASTER AND PUPILS

As the halfway point of the season approached and a hectic Christmas period drew ever closer, Roberto Mancini re-focuses his squad ahead of a crucial period for the club.

Would they maintain their lead over Manchester United and perhaps pull even further clear of their rivals who had a difficult run of games coming up?

CHRISTMAS
CHEER

The players always make a point of
visiting local hospitals around the
festive period to bring smiles, gifts and
autographs to youngsters.
  This trip was to the Royal Manchester
Children's Hospital.

David Silva kept up City's 100% home league record with the only goal in a win against Arsenal at the Etihad

Patrick Vieira sets off on the 2011 Santa Stroll - a particularly damp occasion!
Roberto Mancini starts the event and actor David Threlfall joins in the fun

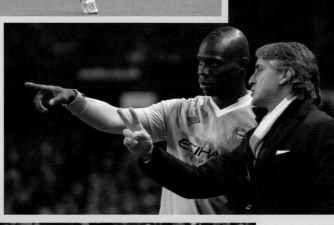

The boys continue to impress with a win over Stoke City

105

Seasonal high spirits

Roberto Mancini raises a glass with journalists at a press conference ahead of the New Year's Day game at Sunderland.

It was a sign of how welcoming he and his staff at Carrington are and it wouldn't be the last time the club enjoyed a celebration that season.

Meanwhile (far left) Mario Balotelli and Samir Nasri play-fight with Nedum Onuoha as the Blues prepare for the trip to the north-east.

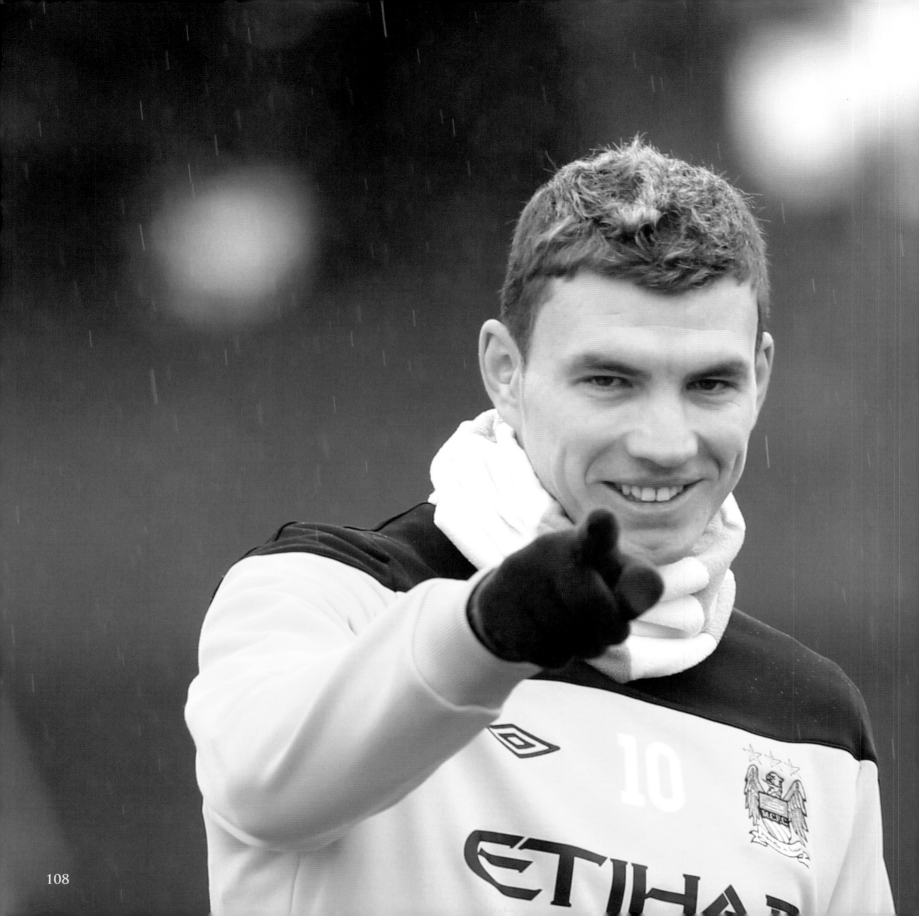

Precious points

Eight games and lots going on behind the scenes meant a very busy January for City, and despite a few body blows in the domestic cups, some big league wins meant there was plenty still to play for

FIXTURES

JAN 01.......PL.......AWAY
SUNDERLAND   0-1

JAN 03.......PL.......HOME
LIVERPOOL   3-0

JAN 08.......FA.......HOME
MAN UTD   2-3

JAN 11.......LC.......HOME
LIVERPOOL   0-1

JAN 16.......PL.......AWAY
WIGAN   1-0

JAN 22.......PL.......HOME
TOTTENHAM 3-2

JAN 25.......LC.......AWAY
LIVERPOOL   2-2

JAN 31.......PL.......AWAY
EVERTON   0-1

Sun Jihai makes a welcome return to Manchester to catch up with a few old team-mates – though only Micah Richards and Joe Hart were around when the popular Chinese defender was last at City

MAN WITH A PLAN

Following a few disappointing results, Roberto Mancini goes over the training schedule ahead of a very busy few weeks.

While the 100% home league record remained intact, the Blues suffered back-to-back domestic cup exits at the hands of Liverpool and Manchester United.

There's a relaxed mood around Carrington as the team
prepare for an FA Cup derby with Manchester United

Behind the scenes at the Etihad everyone – including kit manager Les Chapman – is laid back but on the pitch an early red card for Vincent Kompany didn't help City's cause and they tumbled out of the cup

#ManchesterUnited2-3Home

The eagle eye of Roberto
Mancini is always on the
players as he watches
from a distance

LATE SHOW EXPERTS

Was this the pivotal moment that changed City's season?

The Blues had not been at their best, yet still edged 2-0 ahead against Tottenham who were still very much in the title race.

Goals from Jermain Defoe and Gareth Bale brought Spurs level, and in time added on a Bale cross eluded Defoe's slide at the far post by inches.

Moments later, Mario Balotelli was pulled down by Ledley King and a penalty was awarded – and duly converted by the ice cool Italian to give City a 3-2 injury-time win.

There would be another dramatic victory against London opposition later in the season...

JUST KIDD-ING

Brian Kidd – pictured here with Aleks Kolarov –
is always a popular figure on the training pitch
and, along with David Platt, he is a valued and
vital part of Roberto Mancini's backroom staff.

    The mood was jovial among the players,
but there was still plenty of work to do. As far
as our club photographer's hat goes, the best
Edin Dzeko and Kolarov would give was a
measly four out of ten.

Sergio Aguero reacts with surprise on the training ground, but he's not as alarmed as Edin Dzeko, who suffers a painful moment. Meanwhile, Joleon Lescott shows he's a man of style as he prepares for a photo shoot

Joe Hart tries to reason with a fan who has handcuffed himself to a Goodison Park goalpost

Battle lines drawn

While temperatures plummeted, the title race was hotting up and the Blues threw down the gauntlet, winning every game in February. The emphasis was more on the defence than the offence as City kept a clean sheet in every league game during the month

FIXTURES

FEB 4.........PL.....HOME
FULHAM   3-0

FEB 12.........PL.....AWAY
ASTON VILLA   1-0

FEB 16.........EL.....AWAY
FC PORTO   2-1

FEB 22.........EL.....HOME
FC PORTO   4-0

FEB 25.........PL.....HOME
BLACKBURN   3-0

IT'S FOOTBALL...
BUT NOT AS WE KNOW IT

Joleon Lescott and Micah Richards face off while Nigel de Jong referees as the trio promote Super Bowl XLVI.

The New York Giants triumphed over the New England Patriots with all three featured players – confirmed NFL fans – glued to their TV screens.

126

DAVID DRAFTED IN

David Pizarro was loaned from Roma as Roberto Mancini decided to add experience to his midfield for the final few months of the season.

Mancini knew the Chilean international well from his Serie A days and he soon got into the swing of things as City made February a successful month.

SNOW FALLS AS CITY DRIFT PAST FULHAM

It was a winter wonderland as City took on Fulham at the Etihad Stadium.

So bad was the blizzard at one point, it seemed the game may be abandoned.

Only an heroic effort by head groundsman Lee Jackson and his team – under the scrutiny of more than 45,000 fans – saved the day as the line markings were cleared, enabling the Blues to go on and claim another vital three points.

129

Another EA Sports event at Carrington drew interested spectators who gathered outside of City's training complex. Sergio Aguero obliged the autograph hunters who braved the icy conditions while Adam Johnson and Mario Balotelli prepared for a photo shoot

PASSPORT TO PORTO

Another trip to Europe and a game against Portuguese side Porto.

The Blues flew out from Manchester for a Europa League tie many believed may be a distraction from the Premier League title challenge, but the players were happy to sign autographs as they went.

A kit man's life is not a happy one as Steve Aziz and assistant Brandon Ashton begin the tedious task of unpacking all the players' gear. Meanwhile, the only way is up as far as the Blues are concerned...

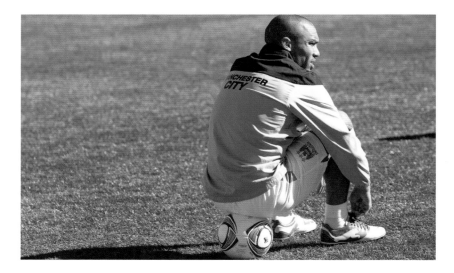

After training on Porto's pitch earlier in the day, the City players had acclimatised enough to beat the Portuguese side on their own patch

Aleks Kolarov and Joe Hart show they're comfortable working the camera on photo shoots, but the City keeper is more at home on the training ground

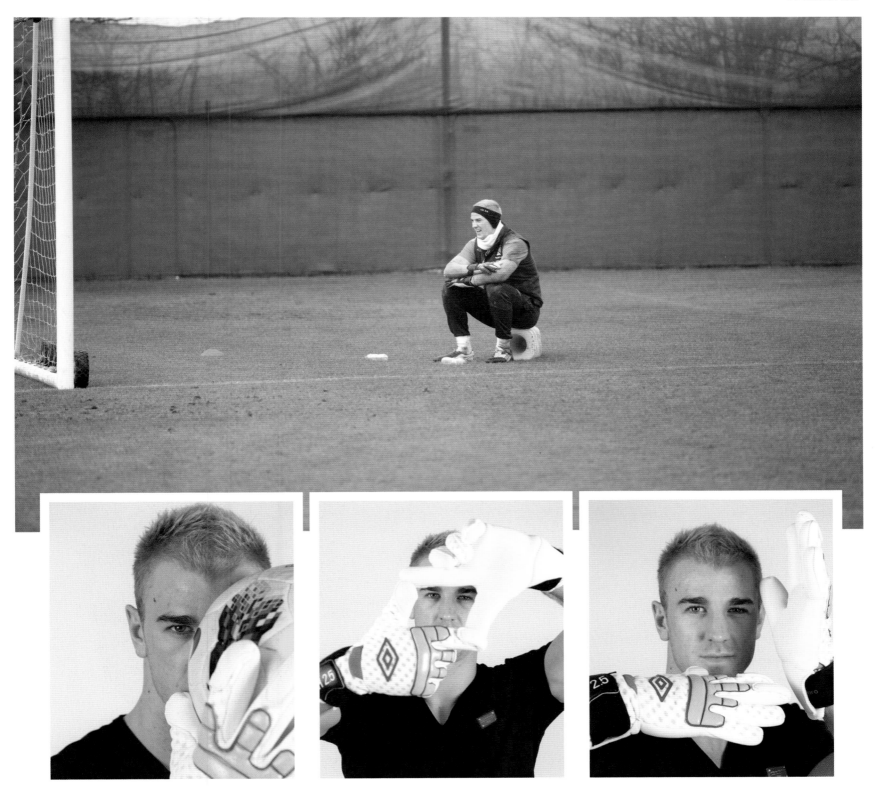

City striker pose

A European trip to Lisbon was a good way to bond as the climax to the season neared. A rollercoaster month saw the Blues eliminated from the Europa League which left full focus on the battle to become champions of England

FIXTURES

MAR 3........PL......HOME
BOLTON 2-0

MAR 8.........EL......AWAY
SP LISBON 0-1

MAR 11.......PL......AWAY
SWANSEA 0-1

MAR 15.......EL......HOME
SP LISBON 3-2

MAR 21.......PL......HOME
CHELSEA 2-1

MAR 24.......PL......AWAY
STOKE CITY 1-1

MAR 31.......PL......HOME
SUNDERLAND 3-3

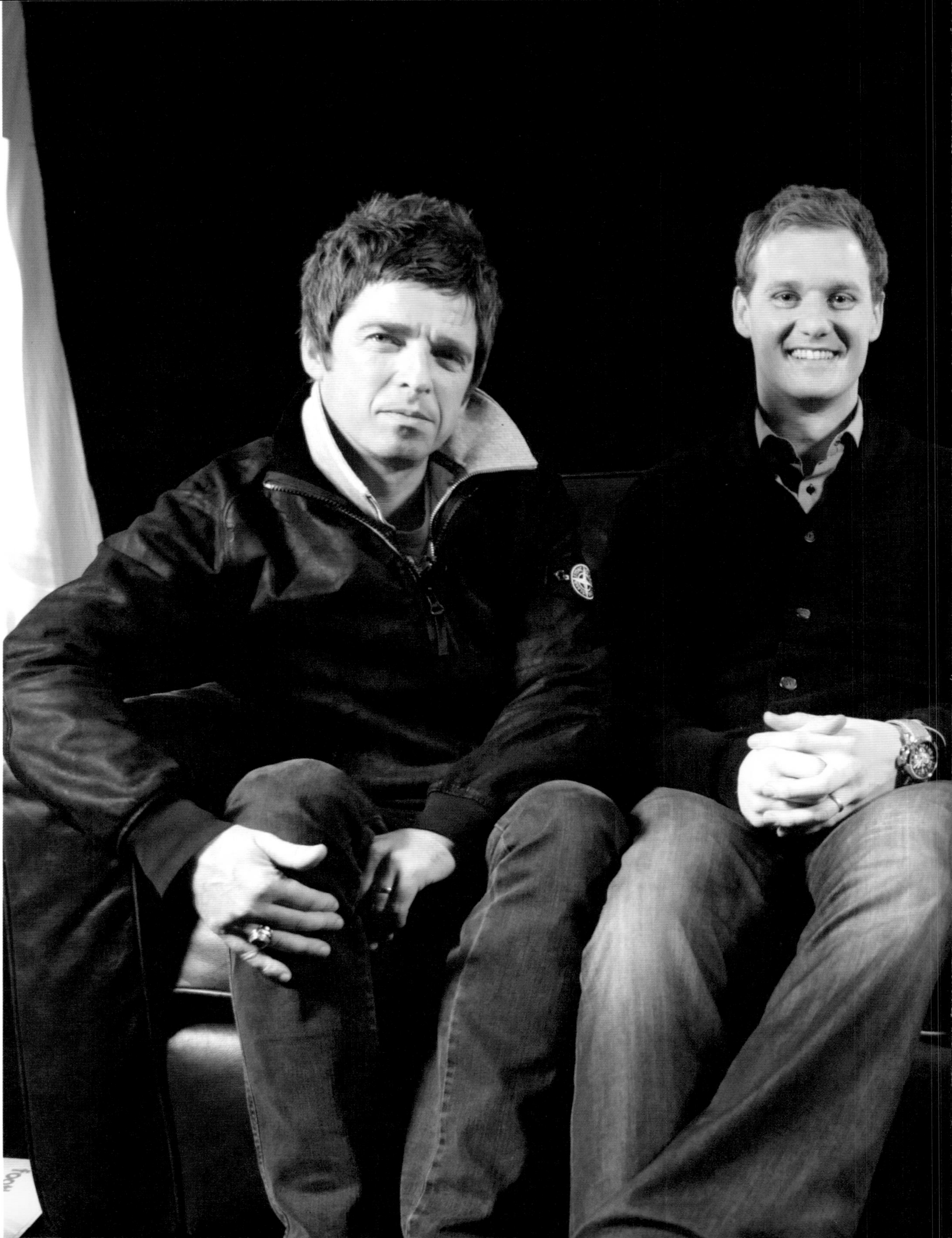

OASIS OF CALM AS MARIO MEETS NOEL

It was the interview that just had to happen – Noel Gallagher and Mario Balotelli.

Both are sitting with BBC sports broadcaster Dan Walker as Noel grilled Mario on everything from penalties to t-shirts and plenty more besides for Football Focus. Pure gold…

Patrick Vieira takes part in CityTV's #askpatrick – a live Twitter Q&A session with City fans

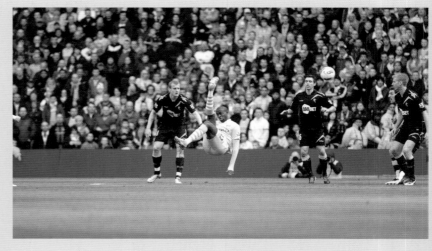

Joe Hart takes the mascots under his wing before he and his team-mates beat Bolton through goals from Gael Clichy and Mario Balotelli

#Bolton2-0Home

Loving Lisbon

City's trip to Lisbon brought some welcome mid-winter sunshine.

As per usual, the squad took a morning stroll along the promenade near their hotel after breakfast.

147

Edin Dzeko shows he's spotted the camera by putting his make-believe glasses on as the players and staff take in the sights of a beautiful European city

#SpLisbon0-1Away

David Silva couldn't help City unlock the
Lisbon defence on a frustrating night

BROTHERS IN TO BAT

The players take part in plenty of events that are rarely heard about or considered newsworthy.

Kolo and Yaya Toure helped promote Sport Relief for local youngsters, while James Milner donned the new Leeds Rhinos shirt – his hometown Rugby League team – and Sergio Aguero took part in the club's new Fan Cam project.

Personalities come to the fore as the squad spot club photographer Sharon Latham in a hotel lobby before the home match with Sporting Lisbon. City won 3-2 but went out of the Europa League on away goals

ONE DAY THIS COULD BE YOU

City's Under-8s are the honoured guests at Carrington where they get to meet the skipper, Vincent Kompany, Gareth Barry and eventually all the squad in a day they will never forget.

BIG GAME PLAYERS

With EA Sports one of the club's partners, it was inevitable that they would turn to the Blues to help promote their new FIFA Street game.

Safe in the knowledge Joe Hart, Joleon Lescott, Nigel de Jong and Micah Richards are all keen gamers, a challenge was set at Carrington. The results are a closely-guarded secret…

A guest of Nigel de Jong, US rapper Drake popped behind the scenes before City's home game with Sunderland but he didn't bring any luck as City's 100% home league record went in a surprise 3-3 draw

Vincent Kompany leads his team out but a point against Sunderland wasn't what City were hoping for

All set for a big finish

The penultimate month of the season was a time for cool heads. After a loss at Arsenal, City went on a run of six consecutive league wins which included the biggest Manchester derby in years. There was still time, though, for some fashion, photo shoots and fun in the community

FIXTURES

APR 8.........PL.....AWAY
ARSENAL   0-1

APR 11.......PL.....HOME
WBA   4-0

APR 14.......PL.....AWAY
NORWICH   6-1

APR 22.......PL.....AWAY
WOLVES   2-0

APR 30........PL.....HOME
MAN UTD   1-0

163

Mikel Arteta's winner for Arsenal had many outsiders believing City were out of the title race

#Arsenal0-1Away

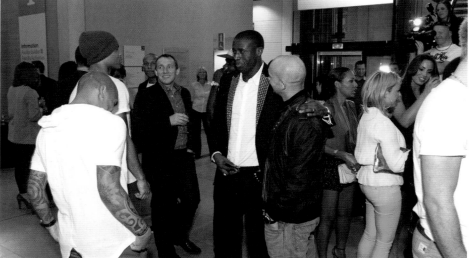

JOLEON'S IN FASHION

Joleon Lescott launches his new fashion label, Lescott-Stewart, in Manchester.

The event is attended by many of the City first-team squad who had seen their title hopes seemingly dealt a fatal blow with a 1-0 defeat at Arsenal.

Mario Balotelli saw red and City were eight points adrift of United with just six games remaining – it looked like mission impossible.

Kitman Les Chapman gathers the tracksuit tops from the players moments before kick-off of the West Brom game

BAGGIES WIN KICK-STARTS RUN

City knew nothing less than six wins out of six would give them a chance of winning the title – but that meant United dropping eight points in their final six games.

The Blues knew their fate was out of their hands yet still delivered a polished display as they beat West Brom 4-0 at the Etihad Stadium.

When news filtered through at full-time that United had lost 1-0 to Wigan, the points gap was down to five…

V FOR VERY COOL

Roberto Mancini had publicly written off his team's chances of catching United, but privately he believed it was still possible.

Prior to the trip to Norwich, he is pictured at Carrington looking very relaxed and focused.

The V for victory sign is what his players needed to deliver at Carrow Road – and they would…

Tracksuit manager Mancini
assesses from afar on a carpet
of a training pitch at Carrington

CARLOS IN THE COMMUNITY

Carlos Tevez returned to City after several months away from the club following a dispute – but with his apology accepted, Tevez embarked on a fitness programme that would see him gradually eased back into the first-team picture.

He was also very happy to attend a City In The Community event at the Etihad Campus Tennis Centre, helping local kids enjoy a varied array of sports.

On the pitch, he was back to somewhere near his best, scoring three goals in the 6-1 thrashing of Norwich as City continued to chase down United.

A Carlos Tevez hat-trick helped Mancini's men to a comprehensive victory at Carrow Road

NORWICH 1 MAN CITY 6

There's no time for a snooze on the training ground, but there's plenty of room for snoods as the City players and manager wear whatever clothing protects them from the elements as April bites

David Silva is interviewed for Spanish TV

Lights, camera, action! Vincent Kompany, Samir Nasri, Joe Hart and Mario Balotelli prepare for the new Umbro kit shoot at Carrington

RELAXED BUT READY

City's 2-0 win at Wolves and United's astonishing 4-4 draw with Everton meant a win over the Reds in the Manchester derby would put the Blues top with two games to go.

The players were focused, very relaxed and believed it was their time. In short, as the players arrived at the Etihad for the much anticipated showdown, there was no way they were about to throw this opportunity away…

179

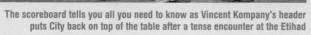

The scoreboard tells you all you need to know as Vincent Kompany's header puts City back on top of the table after a tense encounter at the Etihad

It was Pablo versus Patrice in the battle of the full-backs but the Argentinian came out on top

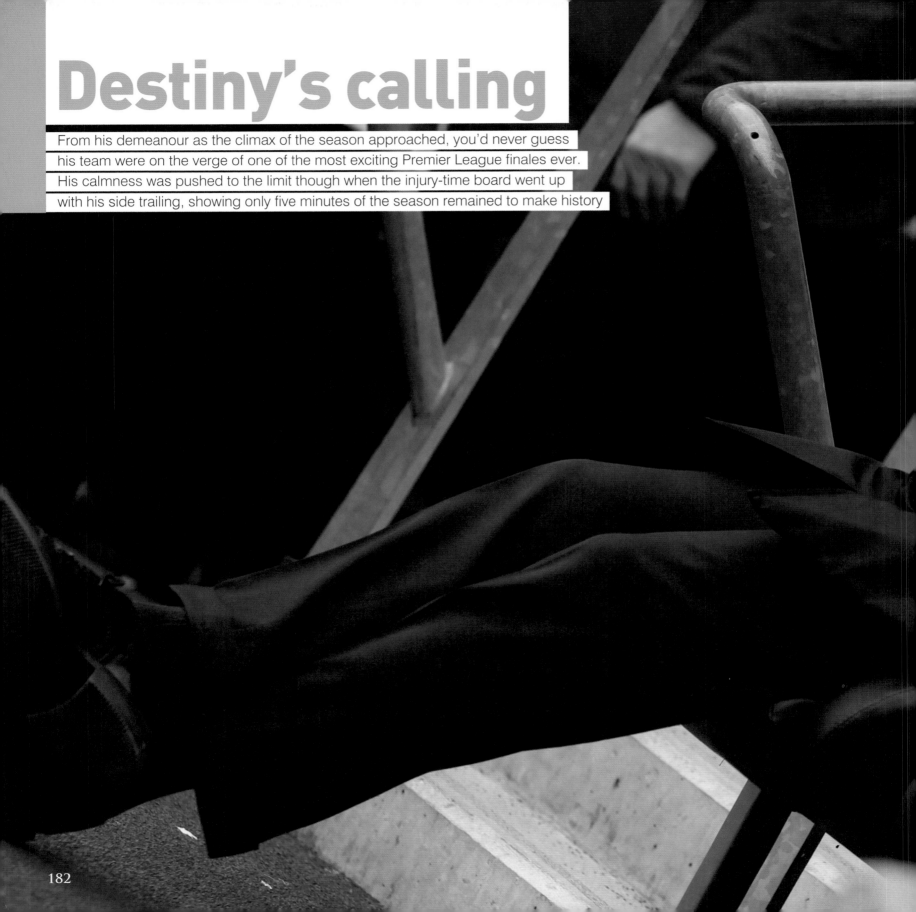

Destiny's calling

From his demeanour as the climax of the season approached, you'd never guess his team were on the verge of one of the most exciting Premier League finales ever. His calmness was pushed to the limit though when the injury-time board went up with his side trailing, showing only five minutes of the season remained to make history

FIXTURES

MAY 06.........PL.....AWAY
NEWCASTLE   2-0

MAY 13.........PL.....HOME
QPR   3-2

CITY IN DISGUISE

Adam Johnson and the majority of the City first-team squad turn out in force for Shay Given's now annual Fashion Kicks event.

Earning large sums of money for charity, the lads enjoy the evening and throw themselves into the action, appearing on the catwalk and taking their mind off the fact they were just six points away from winning the Premier League title.

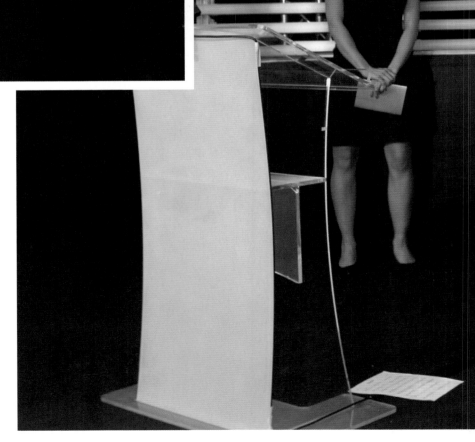

PRIZE GUYS

The MCFC Player of the Year Awards 2012 saw Sergio Aguero voted Player of the Year by the supporters while David Silva picked up the Players' Player of the Year.

Aguero won Goal of the Season (for his effort away to Norwich) and Denis Suarez bagged the Young Player of the Year.

Vincent Kompany won the City in the Community Award and Silva also bagged the EA Sports Player Performance Index Award.

The players don their club suits for the MCFC Player of the Year Awards 2012

Yaya Toure's double at Newcastle kept City in charge of the title race, meaning that a win in the final match the following weekend would almost certainly bring the Premier League trophy to the Etihad

A kick-about with some young City fans for a Barclays promotion at Carrington raises one or two smiles

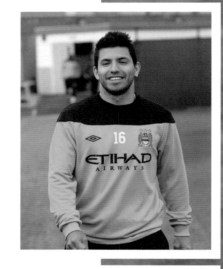

If the City lads were nervous about the final match of the season, they weren't showing it

GETTING DOWN TO BUSINESS

The day finally arrived that City fans had spent a lifetime waiting for – the final match of the season and just three points from a first title in 44 years.

City's 2-0 win over Newcastle the week before had been matched by Manchester United who would go into the final day separated at the top only by an inferior goal difference.

With their rivals at Sunderland, City knew one more big performance should be enough.

The Etihad Stadium was a mixture of excitement, tension and wonder – surely the Blues couldn't let this opportunity pass them by after somehow eating up United's eight-point advantage?

It was nip and tuck with City dominant but QPR dogged. Rangers needed a point to stay up and weren't about to go into the game with a gung-ho attitude

The life of a manager isn't always an easy one and events on May 13 2012
certainly put Roberto Mancini through the mill

HOPES HANGING BY A THREAD

Everything seemed to have been going City's way when Pablo Zabaleta gave the Blues the lead before the break, but Djibril Cisse's equaliser shortly after the re-start suddenly put a spanner in the works.

With City now technically second because of United's 1-0 lead at the Stadium of Light, tensions rose. More so when Jamie Mackie put QPR 2-1 up – this despite being down to ten men following the sending off of Joey Barton.

With 90 minutes played, the board was raised with an additional five minutes to play – surely the title dream was all over?

It's joy unconfined as City level and then go in front through Sergio Aguero
to send pleyers, fans and management into ecstasy

THE IMPOSSIBLE DREAM

Somehow, in the most dramatic finale to the best Premier League season ever, City managed to snatch victory from the jaws of defeat.

It was a quite incredible victory considering what was at stake and the final whistle brought emotional scenes never before witnessed at the Etihad Stadium.

City were champions at long last, but the manner of the victory had made it even sweeter.

An amazing day and the 44-year wait for a top flight title was finally over.

LET THE PARTY BEGIN

The players receive the Barclays Premier League trophy and then enjoy the moment – and why not?

They deserved nothing less after a momentous season where they accumulated 89 points and had an impressive goal difference of +64, eight clear of nearest rivals Manchester United.

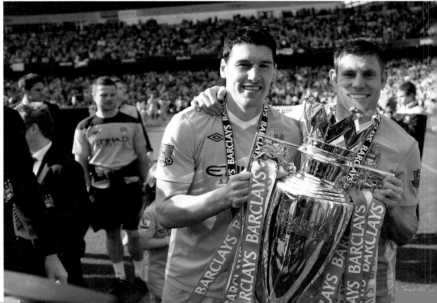

It's all smiles and everyone played a part over the 38 league games – even if they didn't play on the final day

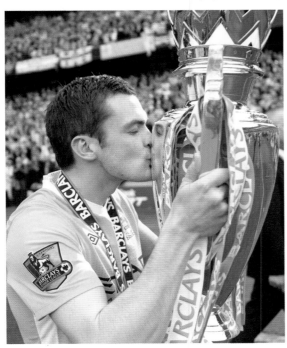

Roberto Mancini has a team shot of his own with several of his backroom staff
– then the party continues, with one or two tears shed on and off the pitch

ACCESS ALL AREAS

Being club photographer means special privileges.

Only Sharon was allowed to take pictures in the champions' dressing room after the match – including the exclusive images on these pages.

It's a case of ice cool Mario as Joleon Lescott dumps an ice bath on the young Italian who played his part in the move that saw Sergio Aguero grab that dramatic winner

215

STREET PARTY

More than 100,000 City fans lined the streets of Manchester city centre to pay homage to their heroes.

The roars were deafening as the open-top bus toured through the city and, fittingly, blue skies ensured it was a memorable end to an unforgettable season.

PARADE OF CHAMPIONS

The club's open-top bus tour of the city kicked off at the Town Hall with the players celebrating on stage in front of thousands of ecstatic supporters.

This was their city – this was their day. Manchester City – Premier League champions 2011/12.

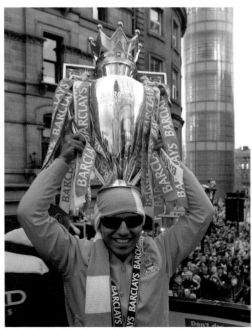

THE PLAYERS AND MANAGEMENT STAFF WHO PLAYED A PART IN AN HISTORIC SEASON FOR MANCHESTER CITY FOOTBALL CLUB:

Joe Hart	Pablo Zabaleta	Roberto Mancini
David Silva	Aleksandar Kolarov	Brian Kidd
Sergio Aguero	Stefan Savic	David Platt
Samir Nasri	Kolo Toure	Attilio Lombardo
Gareth Barry	Carlos Tevez	Fausto Salsano
Edin Dzeko	David Pizarro	Ivan Carminati
Vincent Kompany	Owen Hargreaves	Massimo Battara
Yaya Toure	Costel Pantilimon	
Joleon Lescott	Abdul Razak	
Adam Johnson	Nedum Onuoha	
Micah Richards	Karim Rekik	
James Milner	Luca Scapuzzi	
Gael Clichy	Wayne Bridge	
Nigel de Jong	Denis Suarez	
Mario Balotelli		

The names are too numerous to list individually, but a special thanks to all the backroom coaching staff, the kit team, the medical department, analysis team, kitchen staff and ground staff plus all the people at Carrington, the ticket office and City@Home who all contributed to a fantastic season

Manchester City FC
2011/12 PREMIER LEAGUE WINNERS